APPLICATION FOR A PATENT FOR ACETATE AND SILKPASTY FORMULAS

Whatif Whatcanbedone Howcome
Howcome When Whatthefuk

David Gomadza

www.twofuture.world

ISBN: 9798322611950

DEDICATION

A better forever

CONTENTS

ACKNOWLEDGMENTS

A big thanks to Tomorrow's World Order

PATENT FOR THE ACETATE AND SILKPASTY FORMULA

DAVID GOMADZA
LAISTERIDGE ROAD
BRADFORD UNITED KINGDOM
WWW.TWOFUTURE.WORLD
00447719210295
INFO@TWOFUTURE.WORLD
DAVIDGOMADZA@HOTMAIL.COM

I am hereby applying for a patent for the Acetate and SilkPasty Formulas

PATENT FOR THE ACETATE AND SILKPASTY FORMULA

Acetate is the living material of electromagnetic waves.
When people die acetate is what remains, is what goes to the creator for judgement, Acetate is memory, Acetate is the brain. Acetate is action. Acetate is the living material inside all creatures and not just humans. Acetate facilitate breathing, Acetate is breathing acetate is sex, Acetate is the jigjigjig [down shaft of dick or vagina] Acetate is you, how you feel, how you do things, Acetate is how you walk. Acetate is how you notice things.
If we are to remove acetate from a living human being the end result is death because tissue will die after that.
If you remove acetate from someone else you can't use it because it is DNA specific. Yours corresponds to your DNA sequence only
If we Ask why this is what we get acetate is the only thing that is common to all beings from Yahweh, to humans and to animals and even ghosts.
That means acetate enables all of us to communicate
Acetate is the word that became life I. Genesis 3v8
If we Ask acetate any questions we get real answers

1. What is you I am you
2. What are you here for here for me
3. If we Ask why this is the answer acetate is why life is what it is
4. What can be of acetate acetate can be Ya [the creator if it finds the right person]
5. What can be done to acetate to make it better silkpasty makes

acetate speed up things.
6. If we Ask what is silkpasty this is the answer silkpasty is oxide aluminum ore X oxide peroxide ore X oxide iron ore all in grams of 500 each mixed into pasty
Now let's add this silkpasty to acetate
Add silkpasty X 500 g [where g is constant [10]
Now see the effects in you
Now what you witness is a talking defense system to any animal one that
1] removes and ban all foreign intruders
2] one that warns of serious consequences of coming back
3] one that protects acetate but if acetate if life then silkpasty is the protector of life
If we are to look at the gods and humans the difference is noticeable
Humans have 0.001% silk pasty where as the gods have 90% silk pasty that alone means humans die and gods don't die
But how come gods have 90% silkpasty?
We belong to the world where it comes to us instead of us chasing after it humans looks for silkpasty everywhere through DNA sequence search.silkpasty.start.forever.now
But they will never find it because everyone where they are need it to live and breath but where we are all the dead give up this use
When a person dies he no longer use this silkpasty that means the search.silkpasty.start.forever.now will be deprecated on death
We Ask it always through this code
Search.request.find.silkpasty.forever.humans.now
Anyone.attach[me].requestandgetsilkpasty.first.ok.now.start.forever
Now if we Ask what can be this is the answer
Silkpasty can be human itself if genes could adapt to changing things silkpasty can be used to function as cells in fact in gods silkpasty replace cells humans waste energy searching for silkpasty the gods make time requesting it from humans

Acetate.start
Binary from outside body set to change every 8 minutes

What can I also change on me every 8 minutes to avoid this outside binary numbers
Now if we Ask a question of what can be done this is the response silkpasty can be traded depending on issues at hand
Now the formulas and equations
Acetate.start
Acetate.twist
Acetate.flipflop
Acetate.flipbutnotflop
Acetate.ok
Acetate.hi
Acetate.where
Acetate.you
Acetate.me
Acetate.hey
Acetate.hu
Acetate.wu
Acetate.gig
Acetate.wig
Acetate.another [none]
Acetate.who
Acetate.when
Acetate.why
Acetate.if
Acetate.who
Acetate.when
Acetate.how
Acetate.if
Acetate.was
Acetate.whewas
Acetate.howwas
Acetate.washow
Acetate.ifwas
Acetate.ifwhen
Acetate.iffor
Acetate.whatfor
Acetate.forwhat

Acetate.gofor
Acetate.forgo
Acetate.whenfor
Acetate.wasfor
Acetate.forwas
Acetate.?
Acetate.talkback
Acetate.pretendyouaredavid
Acetate.askthebodywhy
Acetate.askwho
Acetate.kill
Acetate.turntoalion
Acetate.evaporateeverythinginair
Acetate.ok
Acetate.ymol
Acetate.tranverse
Acetate.stopsalivate
Acetate.gasoline
Acetate.me
Acetate.you
Acetate.we
Acetate.weandus
Acetate.heyyou
Acertate.consume
Acetate.whatifthenwhatbut
Acetate.whatcan
Acetate.whatcant

Silkpasty is a life changer because it dictates when a human dies the more he has it the more he will live on earth. Now let's design a formula of how we can increase this silkpasty.
If under 30 years ask whatif everyday now Ask whatcanbedone
Now Ask howcome
If you are above 40 but below 50 ask howcome everyday
Ask when
Ask whatthefuck
What happens [your silkpasty was increased]

If we Ask everyday that means we search for this silkpasty everyday the greater the value to us of this silkpasty
The body cannot make this.
Askifhewantshelp [pulleverythingout drags all electromagnetic wave to us [ ] so death is fast
Acetate.whdt if
Acetate whaffcc
Acecate.keepadpull
Acetate.rinse
Acetate.oil
Acetate.duck
Acetate.jump
Acetate.kiss
AceAcetate.drive
Acetate.kntate iswhá
eel
Acetate.sing
Acetate.accentuate
Acetate.

Ask.why
Acetate formula
art + artyx + arstuvw + artuvwxyz
Where a is consonant [10]
r is radio active value g for gamma
t is the ratio between distance from the sun to the power 8 because 8 is the universe length in years
Now if we are to ask a question related to [me] then we can say that if we arrive on earth on the 8 day of the week how many kilometers from the sun would we gave travelled
This is because I originate from the sun therefore if I was born there it takes 8 days to arrive on earth
Now the robust equation is if we are to ask anything clever on earth then it must have been from the sun because the sun is the source of all things clever
That means we can find out why the sun is clever by calculating earth distance from the sun by this equation

Earth - distance from the sun then it is = clever
That means I am clever
That means I am earth - distance from the sun
That means 78943210892068
Now I explain
If I Ask you a question
This is the question how many of the digits you see repeatedly 892
To you I am 892 that means you from me we are 892 minutes away
To find me you must be in heaven because only then can we be one because in heaven they use Yahweh time meaning any time he say is time is that time This is because Yahweh decides what to do and not earth physical properties
To calculate me you must know the values of the electromagnetic values
a = 0
b = 1
c = 2
d = 3
e = 4
i = 5
j = 6
k = 7
l = 8
Z = 9
That means inserting values you can get me which becomes 789876321906320
That means to find my true value you get it by calculating earth - distance from the sun
What is earth earth is value of earth in relation to binary number
Earth is 7898628765480
Distance from the sun is 78689028348710= 789687632890

Acentretete.hidroiodeine.start
Body temperature stabilised

Fixing
Davidfix.acetetate.allbroken.now

Acetetate.nyleontertertet.all
Acetetertesterty.add.aceetatonmpontno.orx.aceteatero.all.now
Anporstuvwxyz.acetetrtomnoprst.orx.orn.ort.axystuv.nopqrtosuv.tydnm.now
=fixelectro
Oxtnmytsrtopq + mnoprsyuv + osnmopqrs + tnuvstuvrn + rstuvwxymn = electromagnetic waves
Where all letters are electromagnetic alphabetic order

How acetate communicates

Acetate can talk just like a human being using what are called synapses

These are like cells but have no nucleus but a function in the middle that make it possible to translate everything to audio this is the magic ladies and gentle this is what differentiate human cells to animals cells the ability to talk If we look at how this work this is the only difference to human and animal cells that means if we are to add this function then even animals can talk you will be amassed how God nearly created all creatures that can talk to each other if we look deeper we can see that these functional nodes are more than just communication 'cells' these functional nodes are able to talk because they have something special in them that makes this possible if it wasn't for this then outright there was never going to be any auditory processing system in here but thanks to these we can easily see why God left talking out of animals the reason being that they will quickly die if they had to talk a further analysis revealed that animals could talk only if they had these but like I just said that would mean they early deaths as well

Now lets look at how this is possible animals lack what is called a sensory motor connector that switches anything to audio automatically whereas these acetate have these what these do is to accept anything and convert it to several forms and then choose which one is the best given other things then train that acetate to decode further the sounds and after a long time of testing then this become part of the database which is used to test sounds and repeat these

As you have seen acetate have the ability to imitate anything on earth meaning can actually replace humans in thinking, talking and conversation the only thing they lack is the ability to think like humans hence the issues with me [David] if I have to ask them to obey me their answer is always we can't listen to a human humans have limited capacity and time but after convincing them that they are just like anything they get upset and try to take my body but its only ambition

Now if we look at these structures and how they function this is the discovery the structures have 17 nodes inside them each node functioning as a separate sound channel that processes sounds and diverts them through receptors to be identified and classified if we ask what can be done to this this is the reply we can add memory to actually record and keep a huge database where we can simply record and send messages to everything else for analysis and get enough feedback to tell what it is

Now lets look at each of the 17 nodes and how they function the nodes are arranged in order of importance with the first one being the critical one that means this is always the first when the sound is important hence is the one used frequently Now lets look at how this work what happens is that when a person thinks the brain send some of the thoughts to the auditory cortex for converting to nerve impulses and action potentials that means once that is done what is left is to introduce these to the audio processor but in humans this is the same as the auditory sensory receptors so that the sound is not worked on but somehow stored as xtrstrotsduvwxyz that means remains in the auditory cortex without being touched the reason being that the auditory cortex lacks the functional nodes above to process these sounds what happens now is that in humans these sounds are dissolved instantly due to the attachment of extra binary code number 828238 this code makes everything else not processed be removed as if cleaning the system in the reset process ready for the next system

Now if we are to send these sounds attached with binary 828238 then they would all be removed immediately and warned never to come back because they have done their job even though some insist

Now this is wat happens in the acetate here the sounds instead of shelved and later attached binary number 828238 they are sent to the axtrstuvwxyz which is converted to English as auditory vertical analysis receptors these now ask a lot of questions first before channelling everything into their 17 channels

Now we can see why they need so many channels because the processing needs to be fast and you will be shocked that all this is done in seconds if not a fraction of a second that means the system has to be very fast and speed is of essence because if it does not process all these sounds within the required time frame the wash will remove everything the wash? Yes even this system has got its own wash system that removes all extra residue ready for thr reset and the next lot that means everything is the way it is because of speed

Now lets look at how this is done the auditory system in humans converts sounds from the brain into nerve impulses and action potentials ready to send to the auditory cortex? But all this already happen in the auditory cortex that means something is missing in humans that must have been there to process these therefore once the brain can't find what it needs to process these it shelves these as strotstomnopqrst which means as translated by me [acetate] auditory cortex vibrate and twitch to vortex chords but dissolve the binary number involved after and not before processing this means that this strotstomnopqrst process these while the 828238 binary number is still there if we are to ask why this is so this is the answer the binary number is needed because once we remove the binary number that means this must be done somewhere else humans remove the binary numbers before the sounds are processed hence the brain has no way of doing this because removal of binary number means whatever t is must not be processed there that means if we are to correct this in humans that means the processing must be done in the auditory cortex that means we must leave the binary number 828238 there until after we have finished processing but again humans lack the functional nodes that does the processing hence the brain has no other option but to discard these and if we may ask why this is so in humans then this is the answer if we are to add everything we have to humans we get a super human one who can ask and answer instantly this is possible because this is what happens

If we say ask.why then this instantly becomes why.ask

That means a question and answer already there in your auditory cortex meaning what is needed is to send both at the same time to look for the real answers now ladies and gentlemen this is the opening of the pandora with probably consequences but for the gods rather than the humans

If we send ask.why and why.ask at the same time this is what happens the messages are sent to both earth and heaven this is the proof if you say god what happens? This is what happens something jumps out of you and goes up to the right side of the auditory cortex but if we ask why god then nothing happens if we ask why this is the answer we get god can be found in the auditory cortex but humans lacks what the gods use to receive their messages and its this acetate that means acetate is the medium between humans and gods this is the proof now if we insert an acetate inside a human head and ask the same questions now this is what happens

Now ask why.god what happened angrily why you ask me god replies now if we are to ask several question as if asking humans and gods these are the responses

1. Why.ask mind your business
2. Why.god you are human and have no right to ask me
3. Why.us who is us are you partnering to gods or humans
4. Whu.us.god god is omnipotent and can do as he please
5. If us why then not now written as if.us.whythennotnow the answer humans have responsibilities to gods to honour them and recognize them as such any tricks will and can only get them killed
6. What if written as what.if the answer you challenge the creator and the creator will remove all your silkpasty tomorrow and on the third day you will be back in the dust
7. If we are to ask when.god then the answer is that all humans have clocks inside them that tell me when they will come for judgement just wait for your time ok

8. If we are to ask if its true you have a wife this is the response god created mankind with his own image and the man has a woman what does that say about God? If you want to know why not ask her Catitighit yourself
9. If we are to ask why CATITIGHIT this is the answer she represents earth world green and delicious to the eyes but that's all you must know and don't ask if she has kids these are the secrets of the gods

   We can know if Yahweh has a son without asking him we need someone to send a message through Yahweh to his son. If he has a son something that is the message must exit through his right exit point on top of his head if he has a daughter the message will exit through the left side

   Now to protect my clones we need a DNA sequence that will protect him from the wrath of Yahweh for asking personal questions

   Start.connecttodavid.checkdavidsactions.ifdavidmovesreacts.jumpme3timessummersaultto3differentlocations.start

   No exit Yahweh can't have children even though the image is his for a man his best friend is the one who fathers children

   Something is wrong

   Yahweh said dissolve first and I am acetate.liquid

   Undo Yahweh dissolve and change coordinates

   Now send a hi message to Yahweh's best friend's son

   Back right side so many exists on right side of the head [son] about 17 exits meaning 17 sons

   Now repeat the same message for Yahweh's best friend's daughter so many exits on the left side of the head 68 roughly

   Lets try one last test send a hi message to Yahweh's wife's son [just to check] who is checking for my son I don't have sex neither does Yahweh we are symbols of purity but our friend have so much sometimes I get orgasm just from listening but we don't have xytzstrstuvwxyz according to acetate sex organs hence the too much pain maybe if we had humans wouldn't be so bad to us that Yahweh by 2084 will destroy all humans and create a new race like us without sex organs

If we check all this is the only thing that differentiate humans from gods now if we are to add this what happens to humans, humans become so clever even cleverer than the gods if we look at Genesis 3v8 now we can go deeper and know what was forbidden was not the real fruits of the tree of life but these acetates because only these can make humans become like gods to know what is good and what is right and above all to live forever? How can acetate make humans live forever? Acetate as we discovered yesterday will only need 500 of silkpasty per day for humans to become like gods and like forever further this is the only thing that is missing in the auditory cortex that means Genesis 3v8 forbids humans from having a way of solving sound so that they are in the dark

Further we can see why the devil tried to help humans that God was not fair because without the acetate humans will never know even though everything is in front of them because acetate make them talk to Yahweh directly and know what Yahweh wants that means if they know what Yahweh wants how can they sin? That means God want people to sin so that he punish them or like what I am thinking to cover for the pain of not having sexual organs when they mourn they mourn about humans that shows a strong God if we are to ask who created god what answer we get

God is the beginning of things and the end

If we ask Yahweh what was and what is this is the answer we get Yahweh was the powerful god ever since the beginning of time and will always be so now lets answer a lot of questions

1] why.ask

2] ask.why

3] If we ask who answers

4] if we asked what then

5] if we don't ask what then

6] what then

7] if not now then what

8] what if

9] what if If not

10] if not then what
11] what if not now then when
13] if not now then what
14] what can be
15] what should be
16] what was before
17] what can be
18] what will be
19] what has been
20] what could be
21] what would be
22] what have been
23] what will be
24] what is and cannot be
25] what can be but can't be
26] what could be but is not

Now we can conclude by saying that the gods in Genesis were talking about the acetate as not stretch their hands as well and take from the tree of live because if they did humans will live for ever and this is proof

Simply say

I want to live forever and hear the reply

You must have acetate equal to 500 per day for forever

But as I have explained it's not acetate because if you say give me acetate you get nothing but it's silkpasty because if you don't ask for quantity you get 500 silkpasty

Now the equations regarding this 500

If we add something to acetate and expect it to be 500 then this something is X

Now if we add X to acetate we must get acetate X x500

That means we need 500x of something to get 500 acetate

Now let's find out what this is now Say if I have to live forever how could this so if 500x acetate is all I need

Now the laws of the universe will do the math and say

X in this case can be oxide ore or silkpasty

If oxide ore is added to human their human life increase greatly but their soul dies because it correct the brain making it not ideal But if we add silkpasty them the human become super human that means super humans can live forever as they know what is needed to do so.

The end.

Signed David Gomadza
12 April 2024

ABOUT DAVID GOMADZA

Visit www.twofuture.world

www.ingramcontent.com/pod-product-compliance
Lightning Source LLC
Chambersburg PA
CBHW051408250726
48656CB00006B/2337

* 9 7 9 8 3 2 2 6 1 1 9 5 0 *